EDWARD
SNOWDEN

NSA Whistle-Blower

BY MELISSA HIGGINS

CONTENT CONSULTANT
EDWIN M. SMITH
LEON BENWELL PROFESSOR OF LAW,
INTERNATIONAL RELATIONS,
AND POLITICAL SCIENCE
UNIVERSITY OF SOUTHERN CALIFORNIA

Essential Library

An Imprint of Abdo Publishing | abdopublishing.com

abdopublishing.com

Published by Abdo Publishing, a division of ABDO, PO Box 398166, Minneapolis, Minnesota 55439. Copyright © 2017 by Abdo Consulting Group, Inc. International copyrights reserved in all countries. No part of this book may be reproduced in any form without written permission from the publisher. Essential Library™ is a trademark and logo of Abdo Publishing.

Printed in the United States of America, North Mankato, Minnesota
022016
092016

Cover Photo: AP Images
Interior Photos: Andrew Kelly/Reuters/Corbis, 4; John Minchillo/AP Images, 10; Arundel Schools/Splash News/Corbis, 12; Alexander Zemlianichenko/AP Images, 15; Carol M. Highsmith/Library of Congress, 17; Susan Walsh/AP Images, 22; RADiUS-TWC/Everett Collection, 26, 32, 86; Tripplaar Kristoffer/SIPA/Newscom, 29; Kin Cheung/AP Images, 34, 40, 48; Christopher Lane/The New Yorker/AP Images, 42; Marco Garcia/AP Images, 52; Lucian Milasan/Shutterstock Images, 55; Hans Punz/AP Images, 57; Human Rights Watch/EyePress EPN/Newscom, 60, 91; Wolfgang Kumm/EPA/Newscom, 64; Jacquelyn Martin/AP Images, 66; Alex Milan Tracy/ZumaPress/Newscom, 70; Guardian/Glenn Greenwald/Laura Poitras/EPA/Newscom, 75, 85; Manuel Balce Ceneta/AP Images, 76; Wolfram Steinberg/EPA/Newscom, 88

Editor: Mirella Miller
Series Designer: Becky Daum

Cataloging-in-Publication Data

Names: Higgins, Melissa, author.
Title: Edward Snowden: NSA whistle-blower / by Melissa Higgins.
Description: Minneapolis, MN : Abdo Publishing, [2017] | Series: Essential lives |
    Includes bibliographical references and index.
Identifiers: LCCN 2015959726 | ISBN 9781680783001 (lib. bdg.) |
    ISBN 9781680774801 (ebook)
Subjects: LCSH: Snowden, Edward, 1983- --Juvenile literature. | WikiLeaks
    (Organization)--United States--Biography--Juvenile literature. | United States.
    National Security Agency/Central Security Service--United States--
    Biography--Juvenile literature. | Leaks (Disclosure of information)--United
    States--Biography--Juvenile literature. | Whistle blowing--United States--
    Biography--Juvenile literature. | Electronic surveillance--United States--
    Biography--Juvenile literature. | Domestic intelligence--United States--
    Biography--Juvenile literature.
Classification: DDC 363.25/092 [B]--dc23
LC record available at http://lccn.loc.gov/2015959726

CONTENTS

CHAPTER
ONE

SECRET MEETING

As they had been carefully instructed, a man and a woman entered a hotel in the Kowloon urban area of Hong Kong, China. It was June 3, 2013, and they had an appointment to keep with someone they had never met or spoken to before. All they knew was the barest of information the person had revealed to them in encrypted e-mails and chats. He held a position of authority in the US government, which gave him access to documents detailing secret government surveillance—documents he now wanted to leak to the world.

On the third floor of the hotel, the man and woman asked the first employee they saw whether there was a restaurant open. This was a signal to the leaker, who had told them he would be standing nearby, listening. The man and woman then entered a nearby small room and waited on a couch. Into the room walked a thin man dressed in jeans and a white T-shirt, carrying a Rubik's Cube.

Edward Snowden was a bit of a mystery to the journalists who traveled to Hong Kong to meet with him in 2013.

In a scene worthy of a spy novel, the three people had just confirmed each other's identities. The man with the Rubik's Cube was Edward Snowden, age 29. The people waiting for him were journalist Glenn Greenwald, age 46, and filmmaker Laura Poitras, age 49.

Secret Conversations

A few minutes later, the three arrived at Snowden's hotel room. Under Snowden's guidance, they stored their cell phones inside the room's minifridge after first removing the batteries. They shoved pillows around the cracks in the door to avoid being overheard. As a former employee for the top-secret Central Intelligence Agency (CIA), and then for contractors of the National Security Agency (NSA), Snowden knew firsthand how cunning government surveillance could be. The government would not be happy with what he was about to do, and he feared being discovered.

As Snowden explained to Poitras and Greenwald during the next several days, he wanted to go public with a trove of thousands of documents he had accessed and copied to flash drives while working for two NSA contracting companies, Dell and Booz Allen

Hamilton. The documents, he said, proved the NSA was conducting widespread, illegal surveillance of millions of Americans in the United States and abroad, including gathering and keeping records of phone conversations, e-mails, and online activity. He added that he wanted to reveal his identity so he could take responsibility; he did not want anyone else to be blamed.

Greenwald interviewed Snowden for several days, and he wrote five articles that would be published in the British *Guardian* newspaper beginning June 5, 2013—four stories about different NSA surveillance programs and one story revealing Snowden as the leaker.

NATIONAL SECURITY AGENCY

The NSA was established on November 4, 1952, by President Harry S. Truman to decipher coded enemy communications during the Korean War (1950–1953). But NSA-like operations actually began as early as World War I (1914–1918), when the US Army gathered information from foreign radio messages. Then, in the 1940s during World War II (1939–1945), cryptologists, people who use machines to decipher codes, gathered information to help defeat Germany. The agency grew in size and scope, and gradually it became larger than the CIA. With the rise of the Internet, the NSA's activities shifted from cryptography to stopping threats of cyberterrorism, computer hacking, and computer viruses. As of 2012, the NSA had a workforce of approximately 30,000 employees located at its headquarters in Fort George G. Meade, Maryland, and at other sites around the world.[1]

Poitras filmed many of their conversations and edited them into a 12.5-minute video. The *Guardian* posted the video on its website, along with the article about Snowden, on June 9, 2013.

With the release of Snowden's identity came a media frenzy of reporters to Hong Kong, trying to locate the whistle-blower. The meetings with Snowden had to end, or he risked being found and arrested. Snowden left his hotel and went into hiding somewhere in Hong Kong. Poitras and Greenwald left for home. None of their lives would ever be the same.

The Leaker and the Leaks

Who was Edward Snowden? Why did he reveal government

secrets? How did he have access to the documents he copied? Would the leaks hurt national security? These were some of the questions shocked government officials, members of the media, and the public asked in the following days and months as many top-secret documents Snowden leaked came to light. The documents revealed programs in which the NSA had collected phone and online data from millions of customers of telecom and Internet companies. Other

WHISTLE-BLOWERS

Whistle-blowers are corporate or government employees who release confidential information suggesting their employer is involved in some kind of fraud, corruption, or threat to the public. One of the most famous US whistle-blowers is Daniel Ellsberg, a former military analyst. He became convinced the US government was lying to the public about the Vietnam War (1955–1975). In 1969, he handed more than 7,000 photocopies of classified documents to the *New York Times* and other publications.[2] The Pentagon Papers leak helped contribute to the war's end. Ellsberg was tried for disclosing classified documents, but the case was dismissed in 1973. More recently, Army Private Chelsea Manning, formerly Bradley Manning, was sentenced in August 2013 to 35 years in prison for leaking hundreds of thousands of secret defense-related documents to the website WikiLeaks.

Various US laws protect most government whistle-blowers, but not in all situations. For example, members of the military, such as Manning, must follow military regulations in addition to federal laws. Snowden maintains he is not eligible for protection under US whistle-blower laws because he was an employee of a private contractor, not a direct employee of the NSA.

Greenwald, *left*, and Poitras, *right*, left Hong Kong unsure of exactly
what would happen next with the information they had released.

documents showed the NSA had wiretapped world
leaders, conducted cyberwarfare, and even infiltrated
online video games.

Debate about the leaked documents swirled.
Supporters of Intelligence Community programs
believed NSA surveillance was necessary in a post-9/11
world in which terrorists threaten national security.
Privacy advocates believed surveillance without a
warrant and without reasonable grounds was an attack
on privacy and the US Constitution.

Debate also raged about the leaker himself.
Snowden's detractors claimed he was a revolutionary
who wanted to overthrow the US government. James
Woolsey, former director of the CIA, said Snowden

should be prosecuted for treason. To his supporters, Snowden was an idealist risking his future and safety to bring light to a hidden government out of control. An editorial in the *New York Times* stated, "The shrill brigade of his critics say Mr. Snowden has done profound damage to intelligence operations of the United States, but none has presented the slightest proof that his disclosures really hurt the nation's security. . . . he has done his country a great service."[3]

Was he a villain or a hero, a traitor or a patriot? Snowden was reluctant to talk about his past, instead wanting to keep the focus on the documents themselves. But a portrait slowly emerged of a computer genius who never finished high school or earned a college degree—a young man who happily followed in his family's footsteps by working in the federal government. His tech expertise helped him land jobs in government security, where he gained access to secret documents. Snowden made a series of discoveries that led him to believe the government was abusing the people it is meant to protect. Disillusioned with his country's deep reach into citizens' private lives, Snowden was faced with a decision—a decision that would change his life and, quite possibly, change the world.

CHAPTER
TWO

UNLIKELY REBEL

Even before June 9, 2013, when Snowden was first identified as the source of the leaked documents, he feared if he revealed too much about his past, he would come across as arrogant or bring unwanted attention to his family and friends. He also feared that talking about himself to reporters would take attention away from the issues. "I don't want the stage," he told a reporter. "I'm terrified of giving these talking heads some distraction, some excuse to jeopardize, smear, and delegitimize a very important movement."[1] However, in the course of several media interviews, a few facts about his past came to light.

Child of the Suburbs

Edward Joseph Snowden was born on June 21, 1983, in Elizabeth City, North Carolina. He grew up in Wilmington, North Carolina, then moved with his family to Ellicott City, Maryland, when he was nine years old. Edward preferred reading to television,

Snowden at age 14

especially Greek mythology, which he would pore over for hours at a time.

Edward's father, Lon, served as a warrant officer in the US Coast Guard, and his mother, Wendy, was chief deputy clerk in the Baltimore US District Court. They divorced in 2001. Edward's older sister, Jessica, became a lawyer at the Federal Judicial Center in Washington, DC. Like his family, Edward expected to work in the federal government.

Though he was smart—his father reported two IQ tests put Edward's IQ above 145—Edward did not finish high school. A case of mononucleosis kept him out of Arundel High School for nine months. Not wanting to repeat the tenth grade, he completed his general equivalency diploma (GED) and studied computing at Anne Arundel Community College beginning in 1999. He never earned a degree, instead hanging out with friends who shared his passion for computers, video games, and Japanese anime.

Patriotic Fervor

Snowden had been in love with computers since he was a kid, and he began working for a community college classmate who ran a technology business. On his way to

Lon worked in the federal government for several years before becoming a big supporter of his son's case.

the office on September 11, 2001, he was listening to the radio as the first plane hit the World Trade Center during the terrorist attacks. Similar to many Americans, the event changed his life. As the Iraq War (2003–2011) unfolded, Snowden was caught up in patriotic fervor and wanted to help free the Iraqi people from oppression. In 2004, Snowden volunteered for the US Army Special Forces. But during training, he broke both of his legs in an accident and was discharged a few months later.

In need of a job, Snowden passed a lie-detector test and rigorous background check and landed a position as a security guard at the University of Maryland. While attending a job fair, he spoke to a representative from the CIA, and in mid-2006, the agency offered him a job in computer networking in the global communications division at CIA headquarters in Langley, Virginia.

Even though he had not earned a college degree, Snowden's computer skills impressed his superiors enough that they sent him to the CIA's school for technology specialists. He took classes for six months, and then the CIA assigned him to the US mission to the United Nations in Geneva, Switzerland, in March 2007. He told NBC News that he was "trained as a spy in sort of the traditional sense of the word, in that I lived and worked undercover overseas—pretending to work in a job that I'm not—and even being assigned a name that was not mine."[2] His duties in Geneva included retrieving information about the Swiss banking industry. It would be the first time he found reason to distrust the US government.

Snowden's skills impressed his supervisors at CIA headquarters, allowing him to move up within the agency quickly.

Seeds of Discontent

While working for the CIA in Geneva, Snowden was disheartened by the ways CIA agents recruited foreigners with hope for receiving valuable information for the agency. For example, Snowden asserted one agent got a prospective recruit drunk, urged him or her to drive home, and then offered to help after he or she was arrested for drunk driving. In addition, Snowden's job maintaining CIA computer systems gave him access to information about the Iraq War. He was unnerved by the details of torture and warrantless wiretapping he discovered. "The war on terror had gotten really dark," he told an interviewer about that period of history.[3]

Believing the CIA's activities were doing more harm than good, Snowden experienced a crisis of conscience about working for the agency; he considered becoming a whistle-blower at that time. But the CIA relied heavily on spies and he was uncomfortable disclosing secrets that might endanger CIA agents or foreign recruits. Plus, Barack Obama had just been elected president in 2008, and Snowden appreciated Obama's pledge that he would not sacrifice individual rights in the name of

NEED FOR TECHNO-SPIES

The 9/11 terrorist attacks killed nearly 3,000 people on US soil. In the aftermath of the attacks, Americans were frightened and vulnerable, and the government was determined to avoid similar events. As a result, the US Congress fed massive amounts of money into intelligence organizations, including the NSA and CIA. Large chunks of that money went to private defense contractors, such as Dell and Booz Allen Hamilton, who hired—and continue to hire—talented young professionals such as Snowden to get the work done.

The dilemma for defense contractors is that people with technical skills sometimes have beliefs and lifestyles that do not fit well within a government bureaucracy. "There were lots of discussions at NSA and in the intelligence community in general about the acculturation process," Joel F. Brenner, a former inspector general of the NSA, told the *New York Times.* "They were aware that they were bringing in young people who had to adjust to the culture—and who would change the culture." He added that after the 9/11 attacks, "you're going to have some sloppiness and some mistakes." He found it remarkable that the "disloyalty" shown by Snowden did not happened more often.[4]

national security. Snowden was optimistic things would change for the better. But by 2010, after two years in office, it seemed to Snowden that Obama had reversed course on surveillance and was no better than his predecessor, George W. Bush.

In 2010, Snowden was working as a technical expert in Japan for Dell, a company that did top-secret work for the NSA. It was an ideal job for Snowden, because he had always wanted to visit Japan. He worked near Tokyo in an NSA office at the Yokota Air Base, teaching military personnel how to defend their computers from hackers. The position gave him access to new information, such as mass surveillance programs, targeted killings, and CIA drone attacks. He also

WIRETAPS

In 2008, during the Democratic primary for president, US Senator Barack Obama said he would end many Bush-era policies, such as illegal surveillance. In a January 2008 speech at Dartmouth College in New Hampshire, Obama said that under his presidency, the United States would leave behind "wiretaps without warrants."[5] He opposed amendments to the Foreign Intelligence Surveillance Act (FISA) that would allow telecommunication companies to avoid prosecution for participating in NSA wiretap programs. Then, four months later, Obama changed course, saying he would vote for a compromise bill in favor of the FISA amendments. Though the change disappointed many of his Democratic primary supporters, it made him appear strong on defense for the general election.

learned the NSA was capable of following every person in a city by monitoring their cell phones, computers, or other electronic devices. The NSA's surveillance capabilities astounded Snowden, and it seemed to him the organization worked on its own with no oversight from the rest of the government.

Snowden's faith in the US Intelligence Community was slowly eroding. Even so, the community continued to value Snowden's technical expertise. In 2011, he took a job as lead technologist—a computer-problem fixer—at Dell's Maryland office. He worked on the CIA's account. But rather than easing his dissatisfaction with US intelligence, the position soured Snowden even more.

Hawaii: Point of No Return

In March 2012, Dell moved Snowden to its Hawaii office, a dank, underground former torpedo storage facility. The tech position again gave Snowden access to top-secret documents detailing the NSA's surveillance activities. For example, he discovered the NSA was passing retrieved e-mails and phone calls made by millions of Arab and Palestinian Americans to Israeli intelligence, without first removing identifying information. As a result, relatives of those Americans living in Israel-occupied Palestine could become targets.

Snowden was also astonished when he discovered a memo showing the NSA was spying on US political radicals, specifically their habits of viewing online pornography. The memo—written by NSA Director Keith Alexander—suggested the information could be used to destroy the reputations of people critical of the US government. The memo included the names of six individuals who could be targeted.

Snowden believed US intelligence had too much power and too little public oversight. He became increasingly compelled to make the American public aware of what he considered were illegal government activities.

QUIET GEEK

After Snowden was revealed as the man behind the NSA leaks, journalists interviewed people who knew him. Joyce Kinsey, a Maryland neighbor of the Snowden family, said, "He was a quiet guy, kept to himself. He always dressed nice, was clean cut. He just reminded me of a brainiac. I feel terrible for his family." Dr. Angel Cunanan, a neighbor of Snowden and his girlfriend in Hawaii, told a reporter, "They['d] just say, 'Hi' and 'Hello' in the morning. He mentioned that he worked for the government. . . . There was nothing strange, nothing like that."[6] An anonymous friend said, "He was a geek like the rest of us. We played video games, watched anime. It was before geek was cool."[7]

CHAPTER
THREE

THE LAST STRAWS

When whistle-blowers inform on a person or organization they believe is engaged in illegal activity, they often use media partners to leak that information to the public. For example, a military analyst, Daniel Ellsberg, released the Pentagon Papers about the Vietnam War to reporters at the *New York Times* and other newspapers. Army Private Chelsea Manning gave her collection of Iraq War defense documents to the WikiLeaks whistle-blower website. Snowden found himself in a similar situation. If he gathered secret documents, how would he release them? Rather than do it himself, he decided to find partners in the media, people he trusted and who shared his beliefs about government overreach. He wanted to spread the documents to more than one source, so the leaks, once started, would be difficult for the government to stop.

Daniel Ellsberg was a famous whistle-blower who released the Pentagon Papers in the 1970s.

Finding Partners

In December 2012, Snowden anonymously sent
e-mails to journalist Glenn Greenwald. Snowden had
become familiar with Greenwald after reading articles

Greenwald had written about
the wars in Iraq and Afghanistan
and about government
surveillance. When Greenwald
failed to respond to his e-mails,
Snowden e-mailed filmmaker
Laura Poitras in January 2013.
Snowden had seen some of the
documentaries Poitras had made
and knew she was currently
filming a documentary on
surveillance. He had also read
a 2012 article Greenwald had
written for *Salon* magazine
about the problems Poitras
was having at airports after the
US government had flagged her as a possible terrorist.
Based on her work and personal experiences, Snowden
believed Poitras would understand the information he

COMPUTER ENCRYPTION

Encryption is a way to
keep data on a computer
safe, whether the data is
stored on a computer's
hard drive or sent over the
Internet. Encryption software
makes data unreadable by
scrambling it into cipher
text, a secret code that can
be unlocked only with a
personal key. Only the user
and the person receiving
the data know the key.
Encryption can be effective.
A randomly selected,
16-character key could take
billions of years to decode.

wanted to leak. He also thought she could communicate it securely.

Poitras quickly responded to Snowden's first e-mail. After exchanging numerous encrypted e-mails during the next few months, Snowden and Poitras gained each other's trust. Snowden suggested she reach out to Greenwald, and in April 2013, Poitras and Greenwald met in New York to discuss what Poitras had learned. They agreed the individual contacting her—who had

"MY LIFE JUST CHANGED"

In January 2013, Laura Poitras received an odd e-mail. A stranger was asking for her encryption key to send her a confidential e-mail. Curious, she did as the person asked. The stranger promised he or she had sensitive information to share. Before long, the stranger was sending Poitras encrypted e-mail messages about secret surveillance programs run by the US government. Some of the programs were familiar to Poitras, but others she had never heard of. "I thought, O.K., if this is true, my life just changed," Poitras told a reporter. "It was

staggering, what he claimed to know and be able to provide."[1]

Poitras was not Snowden's first choice as a media contact. The month before e-mailing Poitras, he had sent a similar e-mail to Glenn Greenwald, a journalist with the *Guardian* newspaper. But Greenwald ignored Snowden's request, partly because of his confusion with using encryption and also because Snowden's e-mails struck him as too ambiguous. "He kept harassing me," Greenwald said in an interview, "but at some point [Snowden] just got frustrated, so he went to Laura."[2]

Snowden and Greenwald talk through Snowden's findings during their initial meetings in Hong Kong.

still not revealed his identity—was legitimate and they should continue communicating.

Snowden was confident he had chosen the right media partners. "Laura and Glenn are among the few who reported fearlessly on controversial topics through this period, even in the face of withering personal criticism." Snowden told the *New York Times*. He ultimately decided to trust Poitras when "we came to a point in the verification and vetting process where I discovered Laura was more suspicious of me than I was of her, and I'm famously paranoid."[3]

A Big Decision

Although Snowden had grown to trust Poitras by the time they met in Hong Kong, his faith in her was untested. Plus, he had not absolutely decided whether he would become a whistle-blower. He had much to consider. Once the top-secret documents were leaked, his life would never be the same. The government would paint him as a criminal, possibly a terrorist. He might be arrested and go to prison. For the time being, Snowden would gather evidence and weigh his options.

By his own account, Snowden was leading a pleasant life. He was making more than $120,000 a year and living in a comfortable rented house in Waipahu, Hawaii, with his girlfriend, Lindsay Mills.[4] Mills, a performance artist and graduate of the Maryland Institute College of Art, had been living with Snowden in Hawaii since June 2012. She wrote on her blog that he was her "man of mystery."[5]

JOURNALISM IN THE AGE OF SURVEILLANCE

Journalists such as Poitras and Greenwald take extra measures to protect sensitive data. In addition to using strong e-mail encryption programs, they use software that hides the websites they have visited. They limit the use of cell phones, which can show who the caller is speaking to and the caller's physical location. Cell phones can also be used as a listening device even when turned off. To prevent computers from being hacked, they use computers that are air-gapped, meaning the devices have never been connected to the Internet.

Gathering Documents

Like any employee or contractor with top-secret NSA clearance and use of an NSA computer, Snowden had access to critical NSA files. These files included documents detailing NSA surveillance programs. As the top technologist in Dell's Hawaii office, Snowden's access went even further—he had access to everything. Though Snowden has not explained how he gathered documents, experts in the US Intelligence Community assume he used a web crawler—a computer program that searches for, and then copies, files that contain certain keywords. He then saved those document files to portable flash drives.

One area Snowden could not access while at Dell was information about the NSA's global cyberwarfare activity. It so happened that another NSA contractor, Booz Allen Hamilton, had an office nearby that could provide him with that data. In March 2013, Snowden applied for, and landed, a job as a computer infrastructure analyst at the company. While at Booz Allen Hamilton, Snowden was able to confirm the NSA was intercepting and storing vast amounts of US communications without warrants or suspicion

Snowden's position at Booz Allen Hamilton allowed him to trace cyberattacks to and from foreign countries.

of criminal activity. He also discovered the use of computer viruses and stolen foreign secrets in cyberattacks. It was a discovery that would set him on a path toward upsetting his comfortable life.

MonsterMind

Working at Booz Allen Hamilton, Snowden became familiar with the Mission Data Repository (MDR), an NSA information storage facility in Bluffdale, Utah. The 1-million-square-foot (93,000 sq m) building holds a yottabyte of data—approximately 500 quintillion pages of text.[6] Every hour, billions of e-mails, phone calls, text messages, and data transfers are routed through the

CYBERWARFARE

Cyberwarfare takes place when computer technicians or automated computer software programs break into an enemy's computers, an activity known as hacking, to learn strategic information or conduct sabotage. For example, a technician working for the US military might hack into an enemy country's defense systems to learn where their troops are moving and what kinds of weapons they are using. A technician might then sabotage the enemy's missile launch codes so the weapons do not operate correctly. Other examples of cyberwarfare might include shutting down websites or social media sites or disrupting a country's power systems.

MDR. Most communications flow through without stopping, whereas others are kept temporarily or indefinitely.

Snowden thought the massive capture of information was disturbing enough. Then he discovered an NSA cyberwarfare program he considered even worse. Called MonsterMind, the program in development at the NSA would look for suspected cyberattacks, block them from entering the country, then automatically send a cyberattack back to the country of origin. Because foreign cyberattacks are often routed through innocent third countries, that meant an innocent country might be the recipient of a US cyberattack. Plus, for the program to work effectively, virtually every private communication coming from overseas would have to be captured.

Snowden considered this the ultimate invasion of privacy. Speaking to a reporter about MonsterMind, Snowden commented, "That means violating the Fourth Amendment, seizing private communications without a warrant, without probable cause or even a suspicion of wrongdoing. For everyone, all the time."[7]

Then, on March 13, 2013, Snowden read a news account of a statement given the previous day by James Clapper, director of National Intelligence, to a US Senate committee. When asked by a senator whether the NSA collected any type of data on Americans, Clapper responded, "No, sir."[8] Floored by what he considered an outright lie, Snowden made his decision to become a whistle-blower.

Yet he had doubts. "It's really hard to take that step," he said in an interview. "Not only do I believe in something, I believe in it enough that I'm willing to set my own life on fire and burn it to the ground."[9] Though he believed revealing what he saw as government wrongdoing was ethical, he knew the US government would not see it that way. He was especially worried about his family, friends, and girlfriend; he feared government authorities would come after anyone who had known him. The thought kept him awake at night.

CHAPTER
FOUR

HONG KONG

After working at Dell and Booz Allen Hamilton in 2012 and 2013, Snowden turned over approximately 50,000 top-secret documents.[1] His intention was to release the documents to his media partners, who would then release them to the world. With the last puzzle pieces falling into place, Snowden finally stepped into the role of whistle-blower.

Hawaii to Hong Kong

It was May 2013. After copying the remaining set of documents he wanted to disclose, Snowden told his supervisor at Booz Allen Hamilton he needed time off. He said he would be gone for a couple of weeks to get treatment for epilepsy. He was diagnosed with epilepsy in 2012. At home, he packed a bag and told his girlfriend, Mills, he was going on a business trip. He did not reveal the real reason for his trip or his destination, hoping to protect her from government harassment once his identity was revealed.

Although Snowden feared the consequences of his actions, he knew it was time to tell the truth.

Snowden spent his time in Hong Kong reading books, ordering room service, and rarely leaving the hotel.

On May 20, Snowden boarded a plane bound for Hong Kong. He carried encrypted flash drives containing thousands of top-secret NSA documents. Even though China had a reputation for suppressing personal freedoms, Snowden chose Hong Kong because the region had a tradition of allowing free speech. He also thought US intelligence agents would have a harder time operating in China, a country with complicated ties to the United States. He hoped this would make it more difficult to deport him. Though he used his own name and credit cards—not wanting to appear as if he were undercover and draw attention to himself—Snowden stayed in his room at the Mira hotel.

A Plan

From his hotel room, Snowden also continued his encrypted chats with his media partners Poitras and

Greenwald. Snowden sent many secret documents via encrypted e-mail to Poitras and approximately 25 documents to Greenwald.[2] He asked them to come to Hong Kong immediately to meet with him and decide how they should move forward. Poitras and Greenwald agreed, and they arrived in Hong Kong on June 2.

After answering the journalists' questions and mutually deciding they could trust each other, the three came up with a plan. Snowden requested Greenwald release only one document at a time, rather than dump them all at once. He wanted people to fully digest each topic. With the assistance of fellow *Guardian* reporter Ewen MacAskill, Greenwald wrote separate articles about three leaked documents. They would wait to reveal

HONG KONG

Hong Kong, with a population of 7.2 million people, is located in the South China Sea in southeastern China. Once a British colony, it became a special administrative region of China in 1997. China agreed to give Hong Kong a high degree of autonomy under a principle it calls "one country, two systems."[3] The principle lets Hong Kong keep its economic and social systems as they are until 2047. The Hong Kong government is only somewhat democratic, in that citizens are allowed to vote for leaders only on a preapproved list. The region is a major banking and corporate center and has its own currency and trade regulations.

Snowden's name, so the government and public response would stay on the stories, not on the whistle-blower.

Greenwald's first story, published on June 5 in the *Guardian* newspaper, was about a secret NSA program that required the telecom company Verizon to release millions of telephone records. On June 6, the *Guardian*

LAURA POITRAS AND GLENN GREENWALD

The two people who would eventually help Snowden change the future of government became almost as famous as Snowden himself. Born in Boston, Massachusetts, in 1964, Laura Poitras moved to San Francisco, California, after high school. She worked as a chef and studied filmmaking at the San Francisco Art Institute. She moved to New York in 1992, where she began studying documentary filmmaking. Her first film as director was released in 2003. Her documentary *My Country, My Country*, was nominated for Best Documentary at the 2007 Academy Awards. Her documentary about Edward Snowden, *Citizenfour*, won the 2015 Academy Award for Best Documentary. She is based in Berlin, Germany.

Glenn Greenwald was born in Queens, New York, in 1967 and spent his childhood in South Florida. After graduating from George Washington University and New York University School of Law, he began his career as an attorney with an interest in defending civil liberties. In 2005, he quit his law practice and moved to Brazil, where he began writing a political blog.

In 2014, Greenwald and Poitras—along with investigative reporter Jeremy Scahill—founded an online magazine called the *Intercept*, which, according to its website, is "dedicated to producing fearless, adversarial journalism."[4]

published Greenwald's second article about an NSA mass-surveillance program called PRISM. That same day, a different article about PRISM appeared in the *Washington Post*, written by Barton Gellman, a journalist Snowden had previously contacted. Then, on June 8, the *Guardian* published Greenwald's third story, about an NSA data mining tool code named Boundless Informant.

Watching and Waiting

Sitting in his Hong Kong hotel room, Snowden watched television and monitored the Internet as the disclosures emerged. The first article was the lead story on every US national news broadcast. Finally, the debate he had so long hoped to generate was happening; he had no idea whether anyone in the public would care.

But his relief was quickly tempered by threats of prosecution issuing from Washington, DC. President Obama, legislators, Intelligence Community officials, and news pundits were saying surveillance programs were necessary for homeland security. They also said what the leaker had done—stealing top secrets—was highly illegal. The reaction was not a surprise to Snowden, and he expected the US government would

ESPIONAGE ACT

The Espionage Act passed in 1917 to give then-President Woodrow Wilson a way to prosecute dissidents during World War I. It allows for prison sentences and even the death penalty for publishing or speaking about information that might be harmful to the United States or interfere with military operations when the country is at war. Sometimes called the Sedition Act of 1918, it was made less severe under a new Espionage Act passed by Congress during World War II, but many people concerned about civil liberties still believe the act goes too far in restricting free speech.

launch an investigation and say he had broken the Espionage Act of 1917.

An Uneasy Future

As his identity was about to be made public, Snowden worried about his safety. The United States could try to legally extradite him from China. CIA operatives might grab him and throw him on a plane bound for the United States. Or the Chinese government might become involved; seeing him as a valuable source of information, they might capture and question him. "All of my options are bad," Snowden told Greenwald. Snowden at least hoped the publicity of the leaks would give him some safety by making it "harder for them to get dirty."[5]

In the end, Snowden wanted to seek asylum in a country that had no extradition treaty with the United States and that promoted Internet freedom, such as

Iceland. But he had no idea what his future held. He accepted that he might end up in prison. "You can't come up against the world's most powerful intelligence agencies and not accept the risk," he told a reporter. "If they want to get you, over time they will."[6] Snowden would try to put off the inevitable for as long as he could.

On June 9, the *Guardian* newspaper posted Greenwald's article and Poitras's video, revealing Snowden as the person who leaked the top-secret NSA documents. As the three had expected, attention now zeroed in on Snowden. Members of the media descended on Hong Kong trying to locate him. Greenwald and Poitras left the country. With the help of human rights lawyers, Snowden left the Mira hotel and fled to a safe house.

Seeking Asylum

In an interview with the *South China Morning Post* on July 9, Snowden said he wanted the people of China to decide his fate and he would "rather stay in Hong Kong and fight the United States government in the courts, because I have faith in Hong Kong's rule of law." He

Demonstrators in Hong Kong hold signs asking the United States to pardon Snowden and apologize for their surveillance actions.

added he felt safe in the city and planned to stay until he was "asked to leave."[7]

Reports surfaced that Snowden was living at the Russian consulate. Rumors also swirled that he had been having meetings with the Russians, seeking temporary asylum. A spokesperson for Snowden, Anatoly Kucherena, who would later become his attorney, denied the allegations. However, in September 2013, Russian President Vladimir Putin stated Snowden had met with Russian diplomatic representatives while in Hong Kong. And a US government official told a US reporter that on three occasions, Snowden had been seen on closed-circuit television cameras, entering the building where the consulate was located.

Whether he had originally planned to stay in China or go to Russia, it seemed Snowden was working on a number of possibilities for asylum. Ecuador's Foreign Minister Ricardo Patiño told a reporter his government had received an asylum request from Snowden. Snowden received help on his asylum requests from Sarah Harrison, a representative of WikiLeaks. Accompanied by Harrison, Snowden boarded a Russian Aeroflot plane on June 23, 2013. His flight itinerary would take him first to Moscow, Russia, where he had a seat reserved on a plane to Cuba. From Havana, Cuba, he planned to fly to Caracas, Venezuela. From there he hoped to fly to Ecuador, where, if all went well, he would seek asylum and live as a free man. All would not go well.

WIKILEAKS

Australian Julian Assange founded WikiLeaks in 2007 as an online location for whistle-blowers to post secrets without having to go through traditional media outlets. It provides a highly encrypted drop box where people can anonymously post leaks, which are then reviewed by WikiLeaks volunteers. If deemed newsworthy and legitimate, the leak is posted on the site along with an analysis. The US government wanted to find Assange after he released the top-secret defense-related documents Chelsea Manning leaked in 2010.

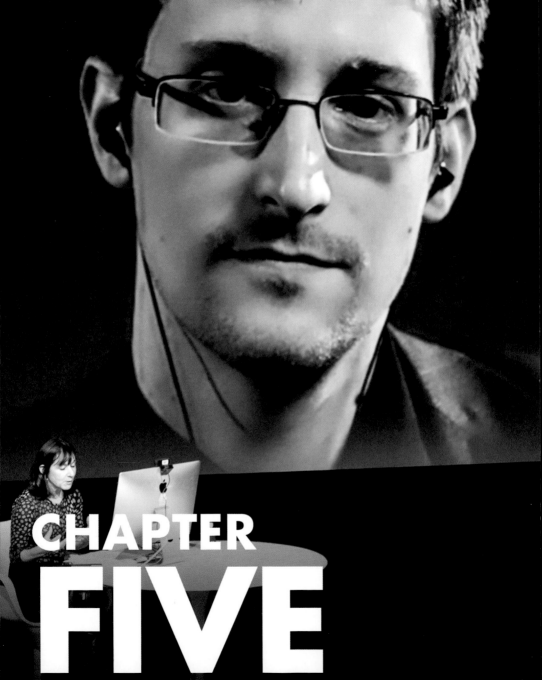

CHAPTER FIVE

LEAK REVELATIONS

S nowden copied documents onto flash drives and turned over approximately 50,000 documents into the hands of journalists. NSA Deputy Director Richard Ledgett said on the CBS news program *60 Minutes* the number was approximately 1.7 million.[1] Snowden says he may have "touched" that many documents, but he actually took far less. During the following months, dozens and then hundreds of leaked documents found their way into news stories. But it was the first three leaks that took the world by storm.

Verizon

The first article about Snowden's NSA documents reveals that, beginning in April 2013, the NSA collected phone metadata, call location, duration, and phone numbers of caller and receiver from millions of American customers of the giant telecom company Verizon. The NSA required Verizon to release information on all US and international phone calls in its systems on a daily basis. The bulk collection program, approved by a Foreign Intelligence Surveillance Act (FISA) court on April 25, 2013, was set to last three months. The approval was unusual because the court typically only allowed data gathering on specific targets or specific groups of targets.

A similar large-scale data mining program had operated under President George W. Bush immediately after the September 11, 2001, attacks on the World

DATA AT THE SPEED OF LIGHT

With the help of private communications firms, the NSA learned how to capture phone and Internet traffic flowing along fiber-optic cables under seas and over continents. Reported by the *Washington Post* in December 2013, one of the documents Snowden leaked showed the NSA could capture this fiber-optic data at the speed of light, taking in the equivalent of "one Library of Congress every 14.4 seconds."[2] The Library of Congress is the largest library in the world, containing 160 million items on 838 miles (1,350 km) of bookshelves.[3]

The NSA collected hundreds of millions of e mail address

books, hundreds of billions of cell phone location records, and trillions of domestic call logs every year. Most of the data belonged to ordinary citizens not suspected of any crime or terrorist plot. The NSA's intent was to map worldwide relationships to find new intelligence targets, people who are not currently on any watch list, a list of people who are considered a threat to US security, but still might be involved in a security threat. The US Congress passed a law in June 2015 ending the NSA's bulk collection of US phone records.

Trade Center in New York City and other targets. But this was the first time the public was made aware of the program continuing under the Obama administration. Even though the content of calls was not part of the data collected, the program allowed the NSA to know who was calling whom, where the callers were located, and at what times the calls were made.

The government deemed the program legal based on the Patriot Act, which was passed in 2001 to strengthen domestic security and broaden the powers of law enforcement to fight terrorism. Specifically, 50 US Code Section 1861 of the Patriot Act allows the Federal Bureau of Investigation (FBI) to collect "any tangible things (including books, records, papers, documents, and other items) for an investigation to obtain foreign intelligence information."[4]

METADATA

Many of the NSA's programs collect metadata, which are the details of a communication, not the content itself. An example of phone call metadata would be the phone number of the caller and receiver, how long the call lasted, and when the call was made. It would not include a recording of the call. E-mail metadata would include the sender and receiver's e-mail addresses and when it was sent, but it would not include the subject or text of the e-mail.

PRISM

On June 6, 2013, the *Guardian* and the *Washington Post*
newspapers published separate articles about another
NSA data-collection program, PRISM. PRISM collected
data on foreign users of Google, Yahoo, Microsoft,
Facebook, YouTube, Skype, AOL, Apple, and Paltalk.
The leaked document was a top-secret NSA PowerPoint
presentation, which showed that more Internet
providers, including the company Dropbox, were
scheduled to be included in the program after 2012.

Unlike the NSA's Verizon program, in which the
NSA requested certain data, PRISM gave intelligence
services direct access to the companies' servers. It
allowed the collection of not only metadata but content
as well, including live chats, file transfers, photos,
videos, search history, e-mail content, and social
networking details. Because it had direct access to
servers, the NSA did not have to get individual court
orders. According to the PowerPoint presentation,
this was the reason PRISM was introduced—to get
around FISA court restrictions. The presentation
claimed, "FISA was broken because it provided privacy
protections to people who were not entitled to them."[5]

Boundless Informant and More Revelations

On June 8, the third article written by Greenwald was published. It detailed a data mining tool called Boundless Informant. The tool mapped, by country, the amount of information the NSA collected from telephone and computer networks. The leaked document showed the NSA had collected nearly 3 billion pieces of communications data during February 2013 alone.[6] A color-coded map showed that most intelligence was gathered from Iran, Pakistan, Jordan, Egypt, and India. The document proved that statements made by the Intelligence Community—that it was impossible for them to estimate how many communications were collected—were not true.

In the following months, many more stories resulting

FISA COURT

In 1978, the US Congress created the FISA court to oversee US Intelligence Community activities and assure their lawfulness. Composed of federal judges appointed by the chief justice of the US Supreme Court, the court is held in secret and most of its decisions are also secret. When submitting wiretap and search warrant requests for approval, the government must show the surveillance target is a foreign power or an agent of a foreign power; it does not need to show probable cause that a crime is being committed.

The *Guardian* slowly reported the surveillance programs
Snowden had found during his years working for the NSA.

from the NSA documents leaked by Snowden were
published in newspapers and magazines around
the world. In June 2013, *Der Spiegel*, the German
news magazine, reported US intelligence agents had
broken into European Union offices in Washington,
DC; New York; and Brussels, Belgium, and planted
surveillance devices.

The following month, the *Guardian* newspaper
revealed details of XKeyscore, a tool used by the NSA
that allowed government analysts to search through vast
troves of e-mails, online chats, and Internet browsing
histories of millions of people without prior approval.

The fall brought more information on secret
programs. In September 2013, the *New York Times*

and the *Guardian* newspapers reported on a leak that showed the NSA was working with private technology companies to weaken the encryption used by commercial Internet companies such as Hotmail, Google, Yahoo, and Facebook. In October 2013, the *Guardian* and the *Washington Post* newspapers revealed the NSA and its British counterpart—Government Communications Headquarters (GCHQ)—had jointly planted malicious code into the computers of people using the Tor network. Tor is a free software program used by businesses and individuals that allows them to use the Internet anonymously. The document showed the NSA was attempting to block access to the network and divert users to more unsecured areas of the Internet.

Another story in the *Guardian* in October revealed the NSA had monitored the

MUSCULAR

The PRISM program, which has its guidelines submitted to a FISA court once a year, was allowed to gather data only on foreigners. To get around this legal block, the NSA partnered with the British GCHQ in a program named MUSCULAR. By breaking into worldwide Yahoo and Google fiber-optic links, GCHQ was able to tap into US communications data. Because the United Kingdom—a foreign country—was gathering the data, the communications they transmitted to the United States were now considered "foreign." The NSA could now legally access the data for hundreds of millions of US accounts gathered by GCHQ.[7]

telephone conversations of 35 world leaders. In a separate story, *Der Spiegel* reported the NSA had tapped German Chancellor Angela Merkel's cell phone.

The *New York Times* reported in November on an internal NSA report asserting US laws were not keeping up with the NSA's need for mass surveillance. The document laid out a four-year plan in which the NSA would eventually be allowed to access data from "anyone, anytime, anywhere."[8]

In December 2013, the *Guardian* released a document showing the NSA was concerned terrorists might be secretly communicating through private chats and web forums of online computer games. The document proposed the surveillance and infiltration of multiplayer role-playing games.

More information on the leaks was revealed in early 2014, too. The *Washington Post* reported in January that the NSA was working to build a quantum computer that

THE FIVE EYES

The NSA leaks revealed a secret communications alliance between five countries known as The Five Eyes: the United States, Canada, the United Kingdom, Australia, and New Zealand. Each of these countries has different laws and rules that govern surveillance. Depending on their intelligence needs, one country might find it useful to use the intelligence data of another member of the Five Eyes or have that country gather the intelligence for them.

could break all types of encryption, including those used by banks, credit card companies, retailers, health-care providers, and governments.

In March 2014, First Look Media revealed an automated NSA system code named TURBINE that could hack into computers, gather data off hard drives, infect computers with malware, record audio from computer microphones, take photos with webcams, deny access to certain websites, and take data from flash drives.

A document released by the *Intercept* in May 2015 described how the NSA has been automatically converting phone calls into searchable text documents. In June 2015, an article published in the *New York Times* and *ProPublica* revealed that in 2012, the Obama administration asked the NSA to step up its hunt for evidence of malicious computer hacking. As a result, the Justice Department permitted the NSA to search Internet cables on US soil without warrants.

The reaction to the initial leaked documents was swift and loud. Although Snowden was pleased they were gaining so much attention, he was now a wanted man and fleeing from a government that wanted to prosecute him.

Edward

CHAPTER
SIX

THE MOST WANTED MAN ON EARTH

As the world digested and debated what it was learning about the NSA's surveillance programs, US government officials were attempting to find Snowden and bring him to justice. The Russian government, other uncooperative foreign countries, and spy-savvy Snowden himself would not make that easy. But the US government's reach was long, and Snowden found his options for asylum dwindling.

Cat and Mouse

After learning the identity of the NSA document leaker on June 9, 2013, the Obama administration scrambled to find Snowden and get him back to the United States. They formally sought Snowden's extradition from Hong Kong. Hong Kong officials said the United States' request did not comply with their laws. The US State

After it was revealed he was the whistle-blower, Snowden had to worry about where he would find asylum.

Department said the extradition request met all necessary requirements, but it still did not go through.

Aware Snowden might be planning to leave China, the State Department contacted countries he might travel to or through. They told foreign diplomatic and law enforcement officials that Snowden was wanted in the United States and should only be permitted to travel back home. The FBI, CIA, the State Department, and other agencies met almost every day, trying to figure out how to capture Snowden. They hoped he would be foolish enough to get on an airplane and fly over US-friendly airspace, so the plane could be forced to land. Snowden was not that foolish. "He goes to the very countries that have, at best, very tense relationships with the United States," US Representative Ileana Ros-Lehtinen told a reporter.[1] Ecuador, for example, had rejected previous requests to help the United States in its attempts to prosecute WikiLeaks founder Julian Assange by letting him stay in its embassy in London, England.

Criminal Charges

On June 14, 2013, the Justice Department charged Snowden with theft of government property, unauthorized communication of national defense

Julian Assange was another whistle-blower
who had difficulty finding asylum.

information, and willful communication of classified
communications intelligence information to an
unauthorized person. The second two charges were
violations of the Espionage Act, just as Snowden had
anticipated. The charges were each punishable by
up to ten years in prison, for a total of 30 years. The
criminal complaint was made public one week later, on
June 21. Two days later, the State Department canceled
Snowden's passport.

Snowden did not learn about the criminal charges or
his voided passport until he landed in Moscow. He had

expected to stay overnight before his flight to Cuba. But without a passport, he was not going anywhere. He was, essentially, a man without a country, stuck in Moscow's Sheremetyevo Airport until he could get special permission from Russian authorities to leave.

US lawmakers were also stuck. How could they get Snowden back to the United States? "It's almost hopeless unless we find some ways to lean on [Russia]," said US Representative Peter King. US Senator Lindsey Graham said, "I hope we'll chase him to the ends of the earth, bring him to justice and let the Russians know there'll be consequences if they harbor this guy."[2] But US appeals to Russia did not have any effect.

In July 2013, Bolivian President Evo Morales was visiting Moscow. On July 2, Morales left Moscow for Bolivia. Thinking Snowden might be onboard the presidential aircraft, the United States alerted Austria, France, Spain, and Portugal to not allow the plane to cross their air space. Austrian officials forced the plane to land in Vienna, Austria, and searched it. Snowden was not onboard, and the incident sparked outrage from Morales and other Latin American leaders.

President Morales expressed his support for Snowden while visiting Moscow, which caused anger among US officials.

Living in the Airport

Snowden would end up spending 40 days in the Sheremetyevo Airport's transit zone. During that time, one of his only connections with the outside world was his lawyer, Anatoly Kucherena. Several times a week, Kucherena would visit the small bare room where Snowden lived. Airport loudspeakers blared for hours on end and the air was stale. "If a person is there indefinitely it can drive him to psychosis," Kucherena told a reporter.[3] Nevertheless, he said Snowden remained healthy, even if anxious about his future.

Though technically a free man, Snowden could not leave the airport without a passport. Kucherena brought books for Snowden to read to help him understand the Russian people, including *Crime and Punishment* by Fyodor Dostoyevsky and Russian stories by Anton Chekhov. He also brought a book on the Russian alphabet to help Snowden start learning the Russian language. Because Snowden had arrived with almost no luggage, his lawyer brought him new shirts and a pair of shoes.

Seeking Asylum

By July 2, 2013, WikiLeaks representative Sarah Harrison, working on Snowden's behalf, had applied for asylum for Snowden in 21 countries.[4] These countries included Austria, Brazil, China, Cuba, Finland, France, Germany, India, Ireland, Italy, the Netherlands, Nicaragua, Norway, Poland, Spain, Switzerland, and Venezuela. None accepted his application. Snowden had earlier made asylum requests to Iceland, Ecuador, and Russia.

In Iceland, Snowden's first choice for asylum, lawmakers proposed a new law to grant him citizenship. But the country said it could consider his request only if he were physically in the country or its embassy. Ecuador had a similar physical requirement. Ecuadorian President Rafael Correa also stated that US Vice President Joe Biden had asked Correa to reject Snowden's

UNBOWED

Believing the United States had put pressure on world leaders such as Ecuador's Correa, Snowden lashed out at the Obama administration for blocking his efforts and for canceling his passport. "These are the old, bad tools of political aggression," he said in a statement issued by WikiLeaks on July 1, 2013. "Their purpose is to frighten, not me, but those who would come after me. I am unbowed in my convictions."[5]

Sarah Harrison, *left*, worked with Snowden, *right*, on his asylum requests.

request. Though it looked as if Russia was Snowden's only realistic choice, he withdrew his asylum request when Russian president Putin said Snowden would have to stop any work aimed at "harming our American partners."[6]

Three Latin American countries, including Venezuela, eventually said they would accept Snowden. But after the incident involving the diversion of Bolivian President Morales's plane, Snowden knew any plane he boarded for Latin America would have to pass over US-friendly skies. He would likely never arrive at his destination. On July 16, 2013, in a press conference at the airport, Snowden again requested asylum in Russia. In his application, he stated he feared torture and the death penalty if he returned to the United States. He also requested temporary, rather than political, asylum. Under Russian law, temporary asylum requires only the approval of the Russian Federal Migration Service, not President Putin.

US Demands and Russia's Response

Responding to this news, the White House again demanded that Russia expel Snowden. "He should return

A WORRIED DAD

Speaking on Russia's Rossiya-24 television news network, Lon, Snowden's father, expressed his gratitude to Putin for protecting his son. Lon said he did not think his son would receive a fair trial in the United States and Russia was the safest place for him at the moment. Snowden watched his father's interview from the airport. Lon was attempting to arrange a visit to Moscow to cheer up his son.

In an earlier interview with the *Washington Post*, Lon said the FBI had asked him to try to get his son to return. But seeing how US Army Private First Class Chelsea Manning, formerly Bradley, also accused of violating the Espionage Act, had been treated, Lon did not have a high level of trust in the US justice system. Manning was "stripped of his clothes," Lon said on Russian television, "kept for 23 hours a day in solitary confinement, his glasses were removed. That was unacceptable." Addressing his son, he said, "I hope to see you soon. But most of all I want you to be safe. I hope you are watching this. . . . Your family is well. We love you."[7]

> "I carefully evaluated every single document I disclosed to ensure that each was legitimately in the public interest. There are all sorts of documents that would have made a big impact that I didn't turn over, because harming people isn't my goal. Transparency is."[10]
>
> —*Edward Snowden, on his careful thinking about releasing the documents*

here to face trial," said White House Spokesman Jay Carney. "He is not a human rights activist. He is not a dissident."[8] In a letter addressed to the Russian minister of justice dated July 23, 2013, US Attorney General Eric Holder formally requested Snowden's return. He assured the Russian government that Snowden would not be tortured or face the death penalty. But US efforts were unsuccessful.

On August 1, Russia granted Snowden a one-year temporary asylum. It could be renewed yearly. After nearly 40 days of confinement, Snowden left the Sheremetyevo Airport and hopped into a taxicab for a secret location. "For the most wanted man on Earth," his attorney Kucherena told a reporter, "personal safety is his number one priority now."[9]

The United States was quick to voice its disappointment with Russia's decision. US Senator Robert Menendez, chairman of the Senate Foreign Relations Committee, said keeping Snowden would set back US-Russian relations. Yuri Ushakov, a Russian presidential aide, said the issue was insignificant and should not affect political relations. The White House canceled a scheduled meeting with Putin because of the incident. One US legislator urged a boycott of the 2014 Winter Olympics in Russia, though the boycott did not take place. For the time being, at least, Snowden had a safe place from which he could watch the world both vilify and celebrate him.

ABANDONED IN HAWAII

Jonathan Mills, father of Snowden's girlfriend Lindsay, said in a January 2014 interview that his daughter was trying to make sense of things and come up with a plan for her future after Snowden left her in Hawaii. She did not realize he was the source of the NSA leaks until she heard it on the news. Mills said the couple had met in 2009 on an online dating site. In July 2014, Mills traveled to Moscow and began living with Snowden off and on; she could not stay permanently because of visa restrictions. She attended the 2014 Academy Awards program in February 2015 and joined Laura Poitras and Glenn Greenwald onstage to accept the Best Documentary Oscar for Poitras's film about Snowden, *Citizenfour*.

CHAPTER
SEVEN

HERO OR TRAITOR?

Just as Snowden had predicted, attention turned to him the moment he was revealed as the person who had leaked the NSA documents. Many people labeled him a traitor and a criminal for illegally stealing secret government documents and threatening national security. Others considered him a hero, willing to risk his future to uncover government wrongdoing. Some believed he should be prosecuted to the fullest extent of the law. Others thought he should be pardoned.

Is He a Traitor?

People who called Snowden's patriotism into question ranged from intelligence officials to politicians to newscasters to corporate leaders. James Clapper, director of national intelligence, said, "This is someone who for whatever reason, has chosen to violate a sacred trust for this country. . . . It is extremely damaging to, and it affects the safety and security of this country."[1]

Although some people viewed Snowden as a traitor, there were many other people who saw his actions as heroic and awarded him and Poitras, *front*, for them.

In 2013, John Kerry, *right*, made it clear to reporters he would not discuss asylum with Russian foreign minister Sergey Lavrov, *left*.

"I read intelligence carefully," said Dianne Feinstein, US senator and chair of the Senate Intelligence Committee. "I know that people are trying to get us. . . . This is the reason the FBI now has 10,000 people doing intelligence on counterterrorism. . . . It's to ferret this out before it happens. It's called protecting America."[2] John Kerry, US secretary of state, said Snowden was a coward and a traitor and that he betrayed his country.

Similar negative views were voiced by news pundits, including Bob Schieffer of *CBS News,* Jeffrey Toobin of the *New Yorker* magazine, and Richard Cohen of the *Washington Post*. Columnists belittled Snowden's background, calling him a loser and a dropout. David Brooks of the *New York Times* mocked his lack of a college degree. Bob Woodward, an investigative journalist who had been a key figure in the Watergate scandal that led to the end of Richard M. Nixon's presidency in 1974, said in a TV interview, "[Snowden] clearly broke the law. . . . I certainly wouldn't call him [a] hero."[3]

Even leaders in the technology industry, those most negatively affected by NSA surveillance programs, were critical of Snowden. Bill Gates, founder of Microsoft,

PUBLIC OPINION ABOUT SNOWDEN

Soon after the first leaked documents were made public, a poll conducted by the Pew Research Center in June 2013 found 54 percent of Americans believed Snowden should be criminally prosecuted, whereas 38 percent believed he should not be prosecuted. A Gallup poll also taken in June 2013 found 44 percent of Americans believed Snowden was right to share documents with the press, whereas 42 percent thought he was wrong to do so.[4]

Five months later, in November 2013, a *Washington Post*–ABC poll showed by a margin of approximately two to one, 60 percent of respondents believed Snowden's disclosures had hurt US national security.[5] A June 2014 poll by Rasmussen Reports, taken after an interview Snowden gave to NBC television, found 31 percent viewed Snowden favorably, whereas 48 percent viewed him unfavorably.[6] A June 2014 *60 Minutes/Vanity Fair* poll found 54 percent of respondents thought Snowden had not acted ethically, whereas 27 percent thought he had acted ethically. Nineteen percent of people did not know.[7]

said in an interview, "I think he broke the law, so I certainly wouldn't characterize him as a hero. You won't find much admiration from me." Marc Andreessen, founder of Netscape, told CNBC, "If you looked up in the encyclopedia 'traitor,' there's a picture of Edward Snowden."[8]

Or a Hero?

Though the tide of opinion flowed mostly against Snowden, he also had supporters. Daniel Ellsberg, leaker of the Pentagon Papers and one of the most famous whistle-blowers in history, posted on his Twitter page, "Edward Snowden has done more for our Constitution in terms of the Fourth and First Amendment than anyone else I know."[9] The Fourth Amendment prohibits unreasonable searches and seizures without a warrant, and the First Amendment guarantees the right to free speech.

Global leaders, particularly those from nations without close ties to the United States, defended Snowden. Nicolás Maduro, president of Venezuela, told a reporter, "How many missiles has Snowden launched against innocent peoples around the world? Has Snowden planted bombs that killed [people?]. . . What crimes has he committed against humanity?"[11]

A petition started on the White House's We the People website gathered more than 100,000 signatures within two weeks after its creation on June 9, 2013. The petition stated: "Edward Snowden is a national hero and should be immediately issued a full, free, and absolute pardon for any crimes he has committed or may have committed related to blowing the whistle on secret NSA surveillance programs." The Obama administration committed to review and respond to any petition that reached more than 100,000 signatures.[12] The White House finally responded in July 2015, not with a pardon but with a call for Snowden to return and face the consequences of his actions. Wrote Lisa Monaco, White House adviser on homeland security and counterterrorism: "He should come home to the United

WikiLeaks created a website to raise legal funds for Snowden in 2013.

States, and be judged by a jury of his peers—not hide behind the cover of an authoritarian regime."[13]

On January 1, 2014, the editorial boards of the *New York Times* and the *Guardian* newspapers urged forgiveness for Snowden. "Considering the enormous value of the information he has revealed, and the abuses he has exposed," wrote the editorial board of the *New York Times*, "Mr. Snowden deserves better than a life of permanent exile. . . . He may have committed a crime to do so, but he has done his country a great service."[14] The editorial board agreed with Snowden's claims that he had taken the only course of action available to him—to expose to the public what he had found and risk the consequences.

Other Avenues of Dissent

In August 2013, President Obama said Snowden could have avoided criminal charges if he had simply told his superiors about the abuses he had become aware of. Obama was referring to an executive order he had recently signed protecting intelligence employees as whistle-blowers. But the executive order did not apply to government contractors such as Snowden.

Snowden also contended that, at various times, he had voiced his concerns. He said he informed NSA colleagues in 2012 about his discovery that the NSA was collecting more

OATH OF SECRECY

NSA Director Keith Alexander and Director of National Intelligence James Clapper said Snowden broke an oath of secrecy, specifically Standard Form 312, the classified-information nondisclosure agreement. Snowden admitted he signed the form, but he has said the oath he chose to keep was to the US Constitution, not a civil contract of secrecy. "That is the oath that I kept that Keith Alexander and James Clapper did not," Snowden said in an interview.[15] He maintained he was not being disloyal to the country, nor was he trying to bring down the NSA; he was working to improve it. Experts counter if this were truly Snowden's belief, he should not have signed the form in the first place.

> "I don't see myself as a hero because what I'm doing is self-interested: I don't want to live in a world where there's no privacy and therefore no room for intellectual exploration and creativity."[16]
> —Edward Snowden

data on Americans in the United States than it was collecting on Russians in Russia. His colleagues were troubled by the revelation but did nothing about it. Earlier, while working in Japan, Snowden said he made recommendations for improving security controls after finding serious flaws with information security. But again, he said nothing was done. Vanee Vines, NSA spokeswoman, said in a statement that after a thorough investigation, including interviews with Snowden's supervisors and coworkers, the agency had found no evidence that he had ever reached out to anyone with any concerns.

Damage to National Security?

One of the biggest criticisms against Snowden was that his actions had severely damaged US intelligence operations. However, no one in the Intelligence Community ever presented proof of harm to the nation's security. Politicians and intelligence officials did report that terrorist groups such as al-Qaeda were changing how they communicated due to the NSA leaks. But the fact that the NSA was aware al-Qaeda had changed its communications procedures meant the NSA was still able to track the group.

Of great concern to the US Intelligence Community was whether Russia or China had been able to access Snowden's cache of documents on his computers. US government officials acknowledged they had no evidence of this, and Snowden insisted he did not expose any files while he was in China and brought none of the documents with him to Russia.

Amnesty or Face Charges?

If Snowden's case were presented to a grand jury for an indictment—a formal charge of a serious crime—the three charges against him could easily increase, so that instead of 30 years he might face a sentence of life in prison. In December 2013, NSA Deputy Director Richard Ledgett considered giving Snowden amnesty if he returned the remainder of the documents that had not yet been published. Ledgett's boss, NSA Director Keith Alexander, did not agree with Ledgett. Not only did Alexander think Snowden should be held accountable for his actions, he did not want to set an example to other people who might do the same thing if they knew they could get the same deal. Plus, any kind of amnesty or plea deal depended on the return of documents, which Snowden repeatedly asserted he did not have.

In a CBS News poll conducted in January 2014, 61 percent of Americans thought Snowden should stand trial in the United States for his actions. Only 23 percent thought he should be granted amnesty.[17] Although public and official opinions were generally unfavorable toward Snowden, there was little doubt the

"WAR" ON WHISTLE-BLOWERS AND A DOUBLE STANDARD

After promising during his campaign that he would protect whistle-blowers, President Obama and his administration proceeded to prosecute government leakers at an unprecedented rate. As of March 2015, eight whistle-blowers had been prosecuted under the Espionage Act. That was more than double the rate of prosecutions of all previous administrations combined.

In 2015, retired general David Petraeus was accused of giving notebooks of classified information, including the names of spies and war strategy, to his mistress who was also writing his biography. Petraeus then lied to FBI interviewers about the facts of the case. He was charged with only a misdemeanor rather than indicted under the Espionage Act. Many consider this a double standard. Abbe Lowell, attorney for convicted whistle-blower Stephen Kim, wrote in a letter to the Department of Justice that high-level officials have been allowed to leak classified information with "virtual impunity."[18]

The leaks made by Snowden made worldwide news
and sparked important conversations.

documents he leaked were having tremendous political

and practical impact.

CHAPTER
EIGHT

THE SNOWDEN EFFECT

I n June 2013, members of the Obama administration
and other US political leaders were focused on
capturing Snowden and bringing him to justice. At the
same time, a groundswell of anger was emerging against
secret surveillance activities, including demands for
change. In what would become known as the Snowden
Effect, changes that resulted from the NSA documents
Snowden leaked would be felt in Congress, the courts,
world capitals, and business boardrooms.

Presidential Panel

In August 2013, President Obama created a panel to
respond to the documents Snowden leaked. Four months
later, on December 18, the panel released a 308-page
report. The panelists concluded that mass-collected
NSA phone metadata had not been proven to be essential
to prevent terrorist attacks. Among the report's

A panel of government officials sits at a Senate Intelligence Committee
hearing in 2013.

46 recommendations, the panel suggested the NSA should no longer store phone data.[1]

The recommendations went further than Obama had said he would be willing to accept. On January 17, 2014, Obama defended the NSA's controversial programs as necessary in the fight against terrorism while acknowledging the outcry over privacy rights. "Threats like terrorism, and proliferation, and cyberattacks are not going away anytime soon, they are going to continue to be a major problem, and for our intelligence community to be effective over the long haul, we must maintain the trust of the American people, and people around the world."[2] In a presidential policy directive, he proposed ending bulk collection of US phone records.

Congressional Response

As early as 2011, two US senators, Ron Wyden and Mark Udall, had been warning the public the US government was using "secret legal interpretations" to use broad surveillance powers the public would be "stunned" to discover.[3] The two Democrats had learned of massive NSA surveillance programs while serving as members on the Senate Intelligence Committee. A few weeks after the first leaked documents were published, two members of the US House of Representatives from Michigan—John Conyers, a liberal Democrat, and Justin Amash, a conservative Republican—introduced the House Amendment Act, a bill to defund the NSA's domestic spying programs. At a time when the two parties agreed and cooperated on very little, their proposal gained surprising support and lost by only a small margin, 205 to 217 votes.[4] Lawmakers said their votes in favor of the bill reflected a concern among voters about personal privacy. "There is a growing sense that things have really gone a-kilter here," US representative Zoe Lofgren told a reporter about NSA surveillance.[5]

On May 22, 2014, a revised and weakened version of the USA Freedom Act was passed in the House by a vote of 302 to 121.[6] The Senate failed to pass the bill in

PAST INTELLIGENCE MISDEEDS

US intelligence organizations have had a history of acting unethically and even illegally. For example, upon discovering in 1963 that Martin Luther King Jr. was having an extramarital affair, the FBI tried to use that information to talk King into killing himself. The CIA tested mind-altering drugs such as LSD on unwitting citizens, plotted to assassinate world leaders such as Cuba's Fidel Castro, and spied on anti-Vietnam War protestors. In the 1970s, US senator Frank Church exposed NSA, CIA, and FBI misdeeds to the public, resulting in reforms such as FISA.

November 2014. The House approved another revised version on May 13, 2015, and it passed in the Senate on June 2, 2015. After the Senate vote, President Obama said in a statement, "Enactment of this legislation will strengthen civil liberty safeguards and provide greater public confidence in these [surveillance] programs."[7] He signed the bill into law later that day. Among other provisions, the act ended mass collection of US phone records by the NSA. Critics of the bill said it would weaken the United States' ability to protect itself.

Court Decisions

In an encouraging win for privacy advocates, on December 16, 2013, US District Judge Richard J. Leon issued an opinion that the NSA's collection of US domestic phone records was probably unconstitutional and violated the Fourth Amendment. In

ALTERNATIVE TO MASS SURVEILLANCE

Even Snowden has said some surveillance is necessary for national security. What he and others concerned with NSA overreach propose is a return to targeted, rather than mass, surveillance. As members of Obama's panel and Judge Leon pointed out, history shows no act of terrorism was ever stopped as a result of mass surveillance. In almost every case where a terrorist act was uncovered and the perpetrators successfully prosecuted, it was as a result of targeted surveillance and investigators interviewing people and following specific leads.

addition, he said the NSA's surveillance capabilities were "almost Orwellian" in scope.[8] He was referring to author George Orwell's book *1984*, published in 1949. He pointed out the government had not cited one instance in which NSA bulk intelligence had stopped a terrorist attack.

Eleven days after Judge Leon's ruling, a federal judge in New York offered a completely different opinion and a win for the NSA. On December 27, US District Judge William H. Pauley III ruled the massive collection of domestic phone data was lawful under Section 215 of the Patriot Act. He argued the program was the US government's "counter-punch" to stop terrorism and did not violate the Fourth Amendment.[9] But in May 2015, a federal appeals court ruled the NSA's practice of collecting data on Americans' phone calls did go beyond

FOURTH AMENDMENT OF THE CONSTITUTION

The text of the Fourth Amendment of the US Constitution, referred to by both judges who ruled for and against NSA mass surveillance programs, reads: "The right of the people to be secure in their persons, houses, papers, and effects, against unreasonable searches and seizures, shall not be violated, and no Warrants shall issue, but upon probable cause, supported by Oath or affirmation, and particularly describing the place to be searched, and the persons or things to be seized."[10]

what was allowed under the Patriot Act. The court said federal law did not authorize the surveillance program.

International and Corporate Response

International response to the NSA's surveillance programs was widespread and frayed some diplomatic relationships with the United States. Germany opened an investigation into the tapping of Chancellor Angela Merkel's cell phone. Brazil was so outraged over NSA spying on its leaders it chose to award a large contract for fighter jets to a Swedish company instead of US company Boeing. Germany and Brazil also voiced a commitment to begin building new Internet infrastructures so Internet traffic would not have to route through the United States. On December 18, 2013, the United Nations General Assembly voted in favor of a resolution affirming online privacy as a fundamental human right.

For US technology companies such as Microsoft and Yahoo, keeping customer data safe is good for business. Conversely, it is bad for business if customers discover their data is being leaked. On December 17, 2013, a delegation of executives from telephone and Internet companies met with President Obama and told him the NSA's surveillance of their networks was a threat to their businesses and the US economy.

When these companies learned, via Snowden's leaked documents, that an NSA program called MUSCULAR was providing back door access to their data without their knowledge, they were enraged. Brad Smith, general counsel of Microsoft, said in a blog post that the NSA posed an "advanced persistent threat," similar to Chinese government-sponsored hackers and

INCREASING USE OF ENCRYPTION

Snowden believes that when strong computer encryption becomes standard and everyone's communications are encrypted, mass surveillance such as that used by the NSA will have to end. Close to one year after the first leaked NSA documents were published, a survey by the network equipment company Sandvine showed encryption usage had increased. In early 2013, before the NSA revelations, 2.29 percent of all peak hour Internet traffic in the United States was encrypted. In May 2014, 3.8 percent of traffic was encrypted. The increase was greater in Europe, growing from 1.47 percent to 6.10 percent. Latin America saw the greatest increase in encryption use, growing from 1.8 percent to 10.37 percent.[11] Some of the jump was attributed to Internet companies using more encryption. For example, in September 2014, Apple and Google announced they were making encryption the default setting for all users. But individual use of encryption was also given as a reason for some of the increase. People were taking other steps to reduce their online footprints, as well, such as clearing their web browser histories.

other online criminals.[12] Corporations even wondered whether the NSA was collecting information about the companies themselves. Smith said in an interview, "For the industry as a whole, it caused everyone to ask whether we knew as much as we thought."[13]

As a result of the leaks, Google, Yahoo, and other tech companies began installing expensive encryption software along their fiber-optic lines to stop mass collection of data traffic. Some Internet companies began routing Internet traffic through other companies' computer servers to decrease eavesdropping. These safeguards meant that if the NSA wanted information, it would have to ask for it through a FISA court or figure out a way to get around encryption one communication at a time.

With companies using more encryption and other technical tools, the Internet was becoming a less user-friendly place for the NSA. Meanwhile, from his home in Russia, Snowden wondered whether the United States would ever be a friendly place for him again.

> "What the government wants is something they never had before. They want total awareness. The question is, is that something we should be allowing?"[14]
>
> —Edward Snowden

The information Snowden leaked caused different responses from people and corporations.

FROM ACADEMY-AWARD®
NOMINATED DIRECTOR
LAURA POITRAS

AND EXECUTIVE PRODUCER
STEVEN SODERBERGH

CHAPTER
NINE

PRESENT AND FUTURE

By August 2015, Snowden had been living in Moscow for two years. Although he said in interviews he felt safe in Russia, he still feared he was being watched and monitored by the US government. He lived a quiet, modest lifestyle, learned a bit of the Russian language, and continued pursuing asylum in other countries. He even hoped to go home someday, even if that meant volunteering to go to prison.

"An Indoor Cat"

James Bamford, a reporter for *Wired* magazine, interviewed Snowden in Moscow in the summer of 2014. Bamford described Snowden as looking thin, almost gaunt, as if his clothes were a size too large. "Overall, he has the look of an earnest first-year grad student," Bamford observed.[1] Snowden said he lived off chips and ramen noodles and spent most of his time

In 2014, Poitras released the documentary *Citizenfour*, which is about Snowden's life.

In 2015, Snowden joined Twitter and quickly became an active participant.

indoors. He referred to himself as "an indoor cat."[2]
Though located times zones away from the East Coast of
the United States, Snowden lived on New York time to
make it easier to e-mail colleagues and watch US news in
real time.

Michael V. Hayden, former NSA and CIA director,
predicted Snowden would become an alcoholic and
waste away in Moscow similar to other Americans
who had defected there. Snowden countered that he
was not a defector, nor did he drink alcohol. To those
who claimed he was being manipulated by Russian
intelligence, Snowden insisted he had no relationship
with the Russian government, nor had he entered into
any agreements with them.

Watching Over His Shoulder

Snowden told reporters he lived a fairly open life without much secrecy. But he also admitted he feared his communications would be hacked by his old employers at the CIA and the NSA. He assumed they were watching him, trying to monitor who he communicated with online. Even with encrypted e-mails, Snowden knew how much information could be gained just from metadata: knowing who he e-mailed and when.

To protect himself and his contacts as much as possible, Snowden continued practicing strict security protocols, such as switching computers often and changing e-mail accounts. He steered clear of shops and restaurants frequented by Americans and Europeans who might know who he was. He instead shopped at out-of-the way places used by locals. When Russians would sometimes recognize him, he would smile.

Invitation to Stay

From his residence in Moscow, Snowden continued to explore his options for asylum. He approached Brazil in 2014, which was still in an uproar over a leaked document that revealed the NSA had monitored the

Brazilian president's cell phone. In an open letter to the Brazilian people, Snowden said he would help Brazil investigate NSA spying in its country. But Brazilian officials said it was highly unlikely Snowden would ever be granted asylum; the country was afraid of jeopardizing its relationship with the United States. Snowden also explored asylum in Germany, France, and Switzerland. In June 2015, French Minister Christiane Taubira said it was possible her country might offer Snowden asylum. But as of December 2015, nothing had come of those requests.

On August 7, 2014, the Russian government announced Snowden had been granted a permit that would allow him to stay in the country for another three years. Snowden was grateful to have a safe place to live for the foreseeable future. In the summer of 2014, Snowden's girlfriend, Lindsay Mills, joined him in Moscow, and they were seen together out on dates. Tabloid rumors swirled the two might marry in Russia, but visa restrictions kept her from living in Russia full time.

Happy to have his girlfriend with him, Snowden nonetheless hoped to go home someday. He even told the US government he was willing to go to prison, as long

There have been reports of Snowden seeking new options for asylum while he has been living in Moscow.

as his imprisonment was not used in a political way; he did not want whatever happened to him to scare other whistle-blowers from standing up for their rights. He did not receive any assurance from government officials that his imprisonment would not be politicized.

Future of Leaked Documents

Snowden said he took none of the leaked documents with him to Russia. Copies—hundreds of thousands of pages worth—an estimated

50,000 documents—were in the hands of news organizations. Those organizations included the *Intercept*, the publishing company started by Laura Poitras and Glenn Greenwald, and newspapers including the *Guardian*, the *New York Times*, *Der Spiegel*, and the *Washington Post*. As of September 2015, approximately 400 of the documents had been published.[3] Alan Rusbridger, the *Guardian's* editor-in-chief, said to the Home Affairs Select Committee about publishing the documents, "We've been working slowly and responsibly. . . . We're not going to be put off by intimidation, but nor are we going to behave recklessly."[4]

Poitras and Greenwald were unsure whether they would ever share all of the documents Snowden gave them:

We have this window into this world and we're still trying to understand it. We're not trying to keep it a secret, but piece the puzzle together. That's a project that is going to take time. Our intention is to release what's in the public interest but also to try to get a handle on what this world is and then try to communicate that.[5]

Reporters speculated that even the NSA did not know exactly what Snowden's massive collection of documents contained. There was also a possibility that leaks were coming from one or more other whistle-blowers and being released under Snowden's name.

OTHER NSA WHISTLE-BLOWER(S)?

Using a sophisticated searching tool, reporter James Bamford scanned all of the documents Snowden leaked. When he could not find some of the documents that had been made public, he wondered whether this pointed toward another whistle-blower—someone else with top-secret NSA access who was leaking documents under Snowden's name.

More evidence for another whistle-blower came in a June 2014 article released in *Der Spiegel*. The article described how the NSA had cooperated with German intelligence. It noted that one of the documents mentioned in the article, an agreement memorandum, was not from Snowden's cache. If one or more whistle-blowers were working for the NSA and leaking documents, it would indicate the NSA had not fixed its leak problem and could not control its own information. "If that's the case," Snowden told a reporter, "how can we as the public trust the NSA with all of our information, with all of our private records, the permanent record of our lives?"[6]

Ongoing Influence

Snowden took heart in the fact that his actions were still influencing public debate and causing political action two years after he met with Poitras and Greenwald in Hong Kong. He was encouraged by congressional efforts to limit mass surveillance and by responses from President Obama and the courts. But Snowden worried the public would become tired of hearing about NSA abuses and simply tune it out. Mostly, he pinned his

SNOWDEN IN POPULAR CULTURE

Snowden's likeness and sayings can be found on T-shirts, posters, pins, bumper stickers, and even cell phone covers. Other places Snowden has appeared in popular culture include:

- *Snowden*, scheduled for release in 2016, was directed by Oliver Stone. It stars Joseph Gordon-Levitt as Snowden and Shailene Woodley as Snowden's girlfriend Lindsay Mills.

- Snowden opened a Twitter account in September 2015. In just a few hours he gained 300,000 followers—more than the NSA, with 76,000 followers.[7]

- *Citizenfour*, Laura Poitras's documentary about Edward Snowden, won the 2014 Academy Award for Best Documentary.

- The animated TV series *South Park* featured Snowden and the NSA in the 2013 episode "Let Go, Let Gov."

- Snowden and government surveillance are featured in the video games *Watch_Dogs*, *Data Dealer*, and *Snowden's Leak*.

- Many books have been written about Snowden, including *No Place to Hide* by Glenn Greenwald.

hopes for reducing unwarranted surveillance on the global use of encryption.

In June 2014, Snowden recalled to a reporter the anxiety he had felt as he had boarded a plane for Hong Kong the previous year. He wondered whether becoming a whistle-blower was worth the risk. "I thought it was likely that society collectively would just shrug and move on."[8] He did not have to worry. His actions riveted the world's attention, triggered an ongoing debate on privacy versus the scope of government surveillance, and prompted changes in how surveillance was conducted. Even if his own future was uncertain, the influence of his actions would be felt for a long time to come.

AWARDS AND HONORS FOR SNOWDEN

- *TIME* magazine's 2013 Person of the Year runner-up
- The *Guardian* 2013 person of the year
- First place in the *Foreign Policy* 2013 list of leading Global Thinkers
- 2013 German Whistleblower Prize
- 2013 Sam Adams Award
- 2014 Nobel Peace Prize nomination
- 2015 Norwegian Academy of Literature and Freedom of Expression's Bjornson Prize for freedom of speech

TIMELINE

1983
Edward Joseph Snowden is born in Elizabeth City, North Carolina, on June 21.

2007
Snowden begins his first overseas assignment for the CIA in Geneva, Switzerland, in March.

2012
Snowden moves to Hawaii to work for NSA contractor Dell in March; he begins communicating with possible media partners to leak secret NSA documents in December.

2013
Snowden retrieves more NSA documents in March when NSA consulting firm Booz Allen Hamilton in Hawaii employs him.

2013
On May 20, Snowden leaves Hawaii for Hong Kong, where he plans to meet with his media partners Laura Poitras and Glenn Greenwald.

2013

Poitras and Greenwald arrive in Hong Kong on June 2 and interview Snowden beginning on June 3.

2013

The first article from Snowden's cache of secret documents—about a secret NSA program involving Verizon—is published in the *Guardian* on June 5.

2013

Two separate articles based on one of Snowden's leaks—about a surveillance program called PRISM—are published in the *Guardian* and the *Washington Post* on June 6.

2013

The *Guardian* publishes an article on June 8 about another leaked document, this one about an NSA data-collection program called Boundless Informant.

2013

Snowden is revealed as the NSA leaker in an article and video published by the *Guardian* on June 9.

TIMELINE

2013

The US Department of Justice charges Snowden with theft and two violations of the Espionage Act on June 14.

2013

The US Department of State revokes Snowden's passport on June 23.

2013

Snowden flies from Hong Kong to Moscow, Russia, and lands at Sheremetyevo International Airport, where he remains in the airport's transit zone for 40 days and applies for asylum in 21 countries.

2013

Russia grants Snowden a one-year temporary renewable asylum on August 1.

2013

US District Judge Richard J. Leon issues an opinion on December 16 that most of the NSA's collection of US domestic phone records is probably unconstitutional and violates the Fourth Amendment.

2013

A panel convened in August 2013 by President Barack Obama to respond to the NSA leaks releases its 308-page report on December 18.

2013

US District Judge William H. Pauley III rules on December 27 that the NSA's massive collection of domestic phone data is lawful under Section 215 of the Patriot Act.

2014

The US House of Representatives passes the USA Freedom Act, limiting NSA surveillance, in a 302–121 vote on May 22.

2014

Russia grants Snowden a three-year residency permit to remain in the country on August 7.

ESSENTIAL FACTS

Date of Birth
June 21, 1983

Place of Birth
Elizabeth City, North Carolina

Parents
Lon and Wendy Snowden

Education
Arundel High School
Anne Arundel Community College

Career Highlights
Snowden was awarded the Sam Adams Award for integrity in intelligence in 2013. Also in 2013, he was named the *Guardian* newspaper's Person of the Year, awarded the German Whistleblower Prize, and received first place in the *Foreign Policy* list of leading global thinkers. Snowden was nominated for the Nobel Peace Prize in 2014.

Societal Contribution
The top-secret documents that Snowden retrieved while working as an employee of two NSA contractors revealed US and foreign surveillance by the NSA on a massive scale. The leaks sparked a global debate about privacy rights versus the need for national security, and they resulted in congressional legislation to place more limits on unwarranted

surveillance—the USA Freedom Act, passed by the US House of Representatives in 2014. Also as a result of NSA activities coming to light, corporations, foreign nations, and individuals began taking measures to evade government eavesdropping, including increasing the use of computer encryption.

Conflicts

Although a majority of Americans believed they had a right to know about the secret programs revealed in the NSA documents Snowden leaked, a majority of the public believes Snowden acted illegally and should be prosecuted. The US government charged Snowden with theft and two violations of the Espionage Act and canceled his passport. Knowing he would be arrested if he stepped foot in the United States, Snowden sought, and was granted, asylum in Russia after applying for asylum in 20 other countries. Many in the US considered him a traitor and a thief and thought he should have chosen a different way to voice his concerns.

Quote

"It's really hard to take that step. Not only do I believe in something, I believe in it enough that I'm willing to set my own life on fire and burn it to the ground."
—*Edward Snowden*

GLOSSARY

anime
A style of Japanese movie and television animation that originated in 1956.

asylum
Protection given by a country to someone who has left his or her country as a political refugee.

bureaucracy
The body of officials and administrators of a government.

consulate
A place where an official in another country works to help citizens from their home country.

cyberwarfare
The use of computers by one country to disrupt activities of an enemy country.

data mining
The practice of searching large databases to gain certain information.

dissident
A person who opposes the official policies of a government.

encryption
The act or process of changing computer data into a secret code so it can be transmitted securely.

extradite
To give up or deliver an alleged criminal to another state, nation, or authority.

malware
Computer software meant to damage or disable computers or computer systems.

metadata
Data that describes or gives information about other data.

mononucleosis
A viral infection with symptoms of fatigue, sore throat, and swollen lymph glands.

surveillance
Watching closely, especially someone suspected of a crime.

telecom
Short for telecommunication, which is communications from a distance, such as by cable or broadcast.

warrant
A document allowing law enforcement to carry out an arrest, a search, or an information-gathering operation.

whistle-blower
A person who informs authorities about an individual or institution he or she thinks is involved in illegal activity.

ADDITIONAL RESOURCES

Selected Bibliography

Bamford, James. "The Most Wanted Man in the World." *Wired*. Wired, 22 Aug. 2014. Web. 20 Oct. 2015.

Broder, John M., and Scott Shane. "For Snowden, a Life of Ambition, Despite the Drifting." *New York Times*. New York Times Company, 15 June 2013. Web. 20 Oct. 2015.

Greenwald, Glenn. *No Place to Hide: Edward Snowden, the NSA, and the US Surveillance State*. New York: Henry Holt, 2014. Print.

Maass, Peter. "How Laura Poitras Helped Snowden Spill His Secrets." *New York Times*. New York Times Company, 13 Aug. 2013. Web. 20 Oct. 2015.

Further Readings

101 Changemakers: Rebels and Radicals Who Changed US History. Ed. Michele Bollinger and Dao X. Tran. Chicago: Haymarket, 2012. Print.

Blackwood, Gary. *Mysterious Messages: A History of Codes and Ciphers*. New York: Dutton, 2009. Print.

Websites

To learn more about Essential Lives, visit **booklinks.abdopublishing.com**. These links are routinely monitored and updated to provide the most current information available.

Places to Visit

Computer History Museum
1401 North Shoreline Boulevard
Mountain View, CA 94043
650-810-1010
http://www.computerhistory.org
The Computer History Museum houses the world's largest collection of computer hardware, software, and other material related to the history of computing.

NSA National Cryptologic Museum
8290 Colony Seven Road
Annapolis Junction, MD 20701
301-688-5849
https://www.nsa.gov/about/cryptologic_heritage/museum
The NSA is a top-secret intelligence-gathering organization and does not offer tours. However, the National Cryptologic Museum, operated by the NSA and located next to the NSA Headquarters, houses a library, gift shop, exhibits, and thousands of artifacts that tell the story of cryptology in the United States.

SOURCE NOTES

Chapter 1. Secret Meeting

1. "NSA 60th Anniversary Flipbook." National Security Agency. National Security Agency, n.d. Web. 21 Oct. 2015.

2. "Pentagon Papers." *Encyclopaedia Britannica*. Encyclopaedia Britannica, 14 Jan. 2014. Web. 21 Oct. 2015.

3. Editorial Board. "Edward Snowden, Whistle-Blower." *New York Times*. New York Times Company, 1 Jan. 2014. Web. 20 Oct. 2015.

Chapter 2. Unlikely Rebel

1. James Bamford. "The Most Wanted Man in the World." *Wired*. Wired, 22 Aug. 2014. Web. 20 Oct. 2015.

2. Erin McClam. "Exclusive: Edward Snowden Tells Brian Williams: 'I Was Trained as a Spy.'" *NBC News*. NBCNews.com, 27 May 2014. Web. 21 Oct. 2015.

3. James Bamford. "The Most Wanted Man in the World." *Wired*. Wired, 22 Aug. 2014. Web. 20 Oct. 2015.

4. John M. Broder and Scott Shane. "For Snowden, a Life of Ambition, Despite the Drifting." *New York Times*. New York Times Company, 15 June 2013. Web. 20 Oct. 2015.

5. Anne Broache. "Obama: No Warrantless Wiretaps if You Elect Me." *CNET*. CBS Interactive, 8 Jan. 2008. Web. 21 Oct. 2015.

6. "What We Know About NSA Leaker Edward Snowden." *NBC News*. NBCNews.com, 10 June 2013. Web. 21 Oct. 2015.

7. John M. Broder and Scott Shane. "For Snowden, a Life of Ambition, Despite the Drifting." *New York Times*. New York Times Company, 15 June 2013. Web. 20 Oct. 2015.

Chapter 3. The Last Straws

1. Peter Maass. "How Laura Poitras Helped Snowden Spill His Secrets." *New York Times*. New York Times Company, 13 Aug. 2013. Web. 20 Oct. 2015.

2. Ibid.

3. Ibid.

4. John Bacon. "Contractor Fires Snowden from $122,000-a-year Job." *USA Today*. USA Today, 11 June 2013. Web. 21 Oct. 2015.

5. John M. Broder and Scott Shane. "For Snowden, a Life of Ambition, Despite the Drifting." *New York Times*. New York Times Company, 15 June 2013. Web. 20 Oct. 2015.

6. James Bamford. "The Most Wanted Man in the World." *Wired*. Wired, 22 Aug. 2014. Web. 20 Oct. 2015.

7. Ibid.

8. Glenn Greenwald. *No Place to Hide: Edward Snowden, the NSA, and the US Surveillance State*. New York, 2014. *Google Book Search*. Web. 21 Oct. 2015.

9. James Bamford. "The Most Wanted Man in the World." *Wired*. Wired, 22 Aug. 2014. Web. 20 Oct. 2015.

Chapter 4. Hong Kong

1. "Snowden Archive." *Canadian Journalists for Free Expression*. CJFE, n.d. Web. 12 Jan. 2016.

2. Janet Reitman. "Snowden and Greenwald: The Men Who Leaked the Secrets." *Rolling Stone*. Rolling Stone, 4 Dec. 2013. Web. 21 Oct. 2015.

3. Peter Harris. "Beware the Hong Kong Democratic Time Bomb." *National Interest*. National Interest, 29 Sept. 2014. Web. 21 Oct. 2015.

4. "Contact Us." *Intercept*. Intercept, n.d. Web. 21 Oct. 2015.

5. Glenn Greenwald, Ewen MacAskill, and Laura Poitras. "Edward Snowden: The Whistleblower Behind the NSA Surveillance Revelations." *Guardian*. Guardian News, 11 June 2013. Web. 21 Oct. 2015.

6. Ewen MacAskill. "Edward Snowden, NSA Files Source: 'If They Want to Get You, in Time They Will.'" *Guardian*. Guardian News, 10 June 2013. Web. 21 Oct. 2015.

7. Lana Lam. "Whistle-blower Edward Snowden Tells SCMP: 'Let Hong Kong People Decide My Fate.'" *South China Morning Post*. South China Morning Post, 15 June 2013. Web. 21 Oct. 2015.

Chapter 5. Leak Revelations

1. Barton Gellman. "Edward Snowden, After Months of NSA Revelations, Says His Mission's Accomplished." *Washington Post*. Washington Post, 23 Dec. 2013. Web. 21 Oct. 2015.

2. Ibid.

3. "Fascinating Facts." *Library of Congress*. Library of Congress, n.d. Web. 21 Oct. 2015.

4. "50 US Code 1861—Access to Certain Business Records for Foreign Intelligence and International Terrorism Investigations." *Cornell University Law School*. Legal Information Institute, n.d. Web. 21 Oct. 2015.

5. Glenn Greenwald and Ewen MacAskill. "NSA Prism Program Taps in to User Data of Apple, Google and Others." *Guardian*. Guardian News, 7 June 2013. Web. 21 Oct. 2015.

6. Glenn Greenwald and Ewen MacAskill. "Boundless Informant: The NSA's Secret Tool to Track Global Surveillance Data." *Guardian*. Guardian News, 11 June 2013. Web. 21 Oct. 2015.

7. Conor Friedersdorf. "Is 'The Five Eyes Alliance' Conspiring to Spy on You?" *Atlantic*. Atlantic Monthly Group, 25 June 2013. Web. 21 Oct. 2015.

8. James Risen and Laura Poitras. "NSA Report Outlined Goals for More Power." *New York Times*. New York Times Company, 22 Nov. 2013. Web. 21 Oct. 2015.

Chapter 6. The Most Wanted Man on Earth

1. James Rosen and Kelly Chernenkoff. "US Revokes NSA Leaker Edward Snowden's Passport, as He Reportedly Seeks Asylum in Ecuador." *Fox News*. Fox News Network, 23 June 2013. Web. 21 Oct. 2015.

2. Ibid.

3. Alec Luhn. "Edward Snowden Passed Time in Airport Reading and Surfing Internet." *Guardian*. Guardian News, 1 Aug. 2013. Web. 21 Oct. 2015.

4. Michael Pearson, Matt Smith, and Jethro Mullen. "Snowden's Asylum Options Dwindle." *CNN Politics*. Cable News Network, 2 July 2013. Web. 21 Oct. 2015.

5. Ibid.

6. Ibid.

7. Sergei L. Loiko. "Edward Snowden's Father Thanks Putin for Protecting Son." *Los Angeles Times*. Los Angeles Times, 31 July 2013. Web. 21 Oct. 2015.

8. David M. Herszenhorn. "Leaker Files for Asylum to Remain in Russia." *New York Times*. New York Times Company, 16 July 2013. Web. 21 Oct. 2015.

9. Sergei L. Loiko. "Edward Snowden Granted Asylum, Leaves Moscow Airport in Taxi." *Los Angeles Times*. Los Angeles Times, 1 Aug. 2013. Web. 21 Oct. 2015.

10. Janet Reitman. "Snowden and Greenwald: The Men Who Leaked the Secrets." *Rolling Stone*. Rolling Stone, 4 Dec. 2013. Web. 21 Oct. 2015.

SOURCE NOTES CONTINUED

Chapter 7. Hero or Traitor?

1. "Director James R. Clapper Interview with Andrea Mitchell." *Office of the Director of National Intelligence*. DNI.gov, 10 June 2013. Web. 21 Oct. 2015.

2. Peter Maass. "How Laura Poitras Helped Snowden Spill His Secrets." *New York Times*. New York Times Company, 13 Aug. 2013. Web. 20 Oct. 2015.

3. Katherine Fung. "Bob Woodward: Edward Snowden Should Have Come to Me Instead." *Huffington Post*. TheHuffingtonPost.com, 20 Nov. 2013. Web. 21 Oct. 2015.

4. Frank Newport. "Americans Disapprove of Government Surveillance Programs." *Gallup*. Gallup, 12 June 2013. Web. 21 Oct. 2015.

5. "Snowden and the NSA—November 2013." *Washington Post*. Washington Post, 20 Nov. 2013. Web. 21 Oct. 2015.

6. "42% Think Snowden Is a Spy." *Rasmussen Reports*. Rasmussen Reports, 5 June 2014. Web. 21 Oct. 2015.

7. "Ethical Dilemmas." *VF News*. Conde Nast, Sep. 2014. Web. 21 Oct. 2015.

8. James Bamford. "The Most Wanted Man in the World." *Wired*. Wired, 22 Aug. 2014. Web. 20 Oct. 2015.

9. Daniel Ellsberg (DanielEllsberg). "Edward Snowden has done more for our Constitution in terms of the Fourth and First Amendment than anyone else I know." 14 Jan. 2014, 1:48 p.m. Tweet.

10. "Few See Adequate Limits on NSA Surveillance Program." *Pew Research Center*. Pew Research Center, 26 July 2013. Web. 21 Oct. 2015.

11. Michael Pearson, Matt Smith, and Jethro Mullen. "Snowden's Asylum Options Dwindle." *CNN Politics*. Cable News Network, 2 July 2013. Web. 21 Oct. 2015.

12. "NSA Leaker Petition Hits 100,000-Signature Threshold in Under 2 Weeks." *RT*. RT, 25 June 2013. Web. 21 Oct. 2015.

13. Maya Rhodan. "White House Responds to Petition Urging Obama to Pardon Edward Snowden." *TIME*. Time, 28 July 2015. Web. 21 Oct. 2015.

14. Editorial Board. "Edward Snowden, Whistle-Blower." *New York Times*. New York Times Company, 1 Jan. 2014. Web. 20 Oct. 2015.

15. Barton Gellman. "Edward Snowden, After Months of NSA Revelations, Says His Mission's Accomplished." *Washington Post*. Washington Post, 23 Dec. 2013. Web. 21 Oct. 2015.

16. Glenn Greenwald, Ewen MacAskill, and Laura Poitras. "Edward Snowden: The Whistleblower Behind the NSA Surveillance Revelations." *Guardian*. Guardian News, 11 June 2013. Web. 21 Oct. 2015.

17. Sarah Dutton, Jennifer De Pinto, Anthony Salvanto, and Fred Backus. "Poll: Most Think Edward Snowden Should Stand Trial in US." *CBS News*. CBS News, 22 Jan. 2014. Web. 21 Oct. 2015.

18. Spencer Ackerman and Ed Pilkington. "Obama's War on Whistleblowers Leaves Administration Insiders Unscathed." *Guardian*. Guardian News, 16 Mar. 2015. Web. 21 Oct. 2015.

Chapter 8. The Snowden Effect

1. Tom McCarthy. "NSA Review Panel Recommends Dozens of New Restrictions on Surveillance." *Guardian*. Guardian News, 18 Dec. 2013. Web. 21 Oct. 2015.

2. Matt Sledge. "The Snowden Effect: 8 Things That Happened Only Because of the NSA Leaks." *Huffington Post*. TheHuffingtonPost.com, 5 June 2014. Web. 21 Oct. 2015.

3. Glenn Greenwald. "NSA Collecting Phone Records of Millions of Verizon Customers Daily." *Guardian*. Guardian News, 6 June 2013. Web. 21 Oct. 2015.

4. Steven Nelson and Tom Risen. "Freedom Act 'Close' One-Year After Amash's NSA Attempt." *US News & World Report*. US News & World Report, 23 July 2014. Web. 21 Oct. 2015.

5. Jonathan Weisman. "Momentum Builds Against NSA Surveillance." *New York Times*. New York Times Company, 28 July 2014. Web. 21 Oct. 2015.

6. Tom Risen. "Freedom Act Passes House After Compromises." *US News & World Report*. US News & World Report, 21 May 2014. Web. 21 Oct. 2015.

7. Bill Chappell. "Senate Approves USA Freedom Act, Obama Signs It, After Amendments Fail." *NPR*. National Public Radio, 2 June 2015. Web. 21 Oct. 2015.

8. Barton Gellman. "Edward Snowden, After Months of NSA Revelations, Says His Mission's Accomplished." *Washington Post*. Washington Post, 23 Dec. 2013. Web. 21 Oct. 2015.

9. Sari Horwitz. "NSA Collection of Phone Data is Lawful, Federal Judge Rules." *Washington Post*. Washington Post, 27 Dec. 2013. Web. 21 Oct. 2015.

10. "Fourth Amendment." *Cornell University Law School*. Legal Information Institute, n.d. Web. 21 Oct. 2015.

11. Klint Finley. "Encrypted Web Traffic More than Doubles after NSA Revelations." *Wired*. Wired, 16 May 2014. Web. 21 Oct. 2015.

12. Brad Smith. "Protecting Customer Data From Government Snooping." *Microsoft*. Microsoft Corporation, 4 Dec. 2013. Web. 21 Oct. 2015.

13. Barton Gellman. "Edward Snowden, After Months of NSA Revelations, Says His Mission's Accomplished." *Washington Post*. Washington Post, 23 Dec. 2013. Web. 21 Oct. 2015.

14. Ibid.

Chapter 9. Present and Future

1. James Bamford. "The Most Wanted Man in the World." *Wired*. Wired, 22 Aug. 2014. Web. 20 Oct. 2015.

2. Barton Gellman. "Edward Snowden, After Months of NSA Revelations, Says His Mission's Accomplished." *Washington Post*. Washington Post, 23 Dec. 2013. Web. 21 Oct. 2015.

3. "Snowden Archive." *International Civil Liberties Monitoring Group*. International Civil Liberties Monitoring Group, 2015. Web. 21 Oct. 2015.

4. "Only 1% of Snowden Files Published—Guardian Editor." *BBC News*. BBC, 3 Dec. 2013. Web. 21 Oct. 2015.

5. Peter Maass. "How Laura Poitras Helped Snowden Spill His Secrets." *New York Times*. New York Times Company, 13 Aug. 2013. Web. 20 Oct. 2015.

6. James Bamford. "The Most Wanted Man in the World." *Wired*. Wired, 22 Aug. 2014. Web. 20 Oct. 2015.

7. Matt Pearce. "Edward Snowden Joins Twitter, Immediately Gets More Followers Than NSA." *Los Angeles Times*. Los Angeles Times, 29 Sept. 2015. Web. 21 Oct. 2015.

8. James Bamford. "The Most Wanted Man in the World." *Wired*. Wired, 22 Aug. 2014. Web. 20 Oct. 2015.

INDEX

ABOUT THE AUTHOR

Melissa Higgins writes fiction and nonfiction for children and young adults. Two of her novels for struggling readers, *Bi-Normal* and *I'm Just Me*, won silver medals in the Independent Publisher (IPPY) Book Awards. Higgins's nearly 40 nonfiction titles range from character development and psychology to history and biographies. Before becoming a full-time writer, she worked as a school counselor and had a private counseling practice. When she is not writing, Higgins enjoys hiking and taking photographs in the Arizona desert where she lives with her husband.